HAL•LEONARD®
GUITAR PLAY-ALONG

AUDIO ACCESS INCLUDED

PLAYBACK+
Speed • Pitch • Balance • Loop

VOL. 21

T0087265

PLAYBACK+
Speed • Pitch • Balance • Loop

To access audio, visit:
www.halleonard.com/mylibrary

Enter Code
5970-2397-8469-4520

Cover photo by Joshua N. Timmermans

 **Hal•Leonard®**

For all works contained herein:
Unauthorized copying, arranging, adapting, recording, Internet posting, public performance,
or other distribution of the music in this publication is an infringement of copyright.
Infringers are liable under the law.

Visit Hal Leonard Online at
www.halleonard.com

Contact us:
Hal Leonard
7777 West Bluemound Road
Milwaukee, WI 53213
Email: info@halleonard.com

In Europe, contact:
Hal Leonard Europe Limited
42 Wigmore Street
Marylebone, London, W1U 2RN
Email: info@halleonardeurope.com

In Australia, contact:
Hal Leonard Australia Pty. Ltd.
4 Lentara Court
Cheltenham, Victoria, 3192 Australia
Email: info@halleonard.com.au

CONTENTS

GUITAR NOTATION LEGEND

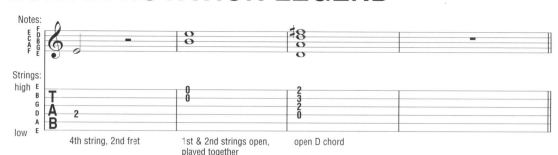

THE MUSICAL STAFF shows pitches and rhythms and is divided by bar lines into measures. Pitches are named after the first seven letters of the alphabet.

TABLATURE graphically represents the guitar fingerboard. Each horizontal line represents a string, and each number represents a fret.

4th string, 2nd fret   1st & 2nd strings open, played together   open D chord

HALF-STEP BEND: Strike the note and bend up 1/2 step.

WHOLE-STEP BEND: Strike the note and bend up one step.

GRACE NOTE BEND: Strike the note and immediately bend up as indicated.

SLIGHT (MICROTONE) BEND: Strike the note and bend up 1/4 step.

BEND AND RELEASE: Strike the note and bend up as indicated, then release back to the original note. Only the first note is struck.

PRE-BEND: Bend the note as indicated, then strike it.

VIBRATO: The string is vibrated by rapidly bending and releasing the note with the fretting hand.

PALM MUTING: The note is partially muted by the pick hand lightly touching the string(s) just before the bridge.

HAMMER-ON: Strike the first (lower) note with one finger, then sound the higher note (on the same string) with another finger by fretting it without picking.

PULL-OFF: Place both fingers on the notes to be sounded. Strike the first note and without picking, pull the finger off to sound the second (lower) note.

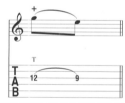

LEGATO SLIDE: Strike the first note and then slide the same fret-hand finger up or down to the second note. The second note is not struck.

SHIFT SLIDE: Same as legato slide, except the second note is struck.

TRILL: Very rapidly alternate between the notes indicated by continuously hammering on and pulling off.

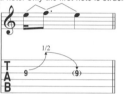

TAPPING: Hammer ("tap") the fret indicated with the pick-hand index or middle finger and pull off to the note fretted by the fret hand.

NATURAL HARMONIC: Strike the note while the fret-hand lightly touches the string directly over the fret indicated.

PINCH HARMONIC: The note is fretted normally and a harmonic is produced by adding the edge of the thumb or the tip of the index finger of the pick hand to the normal pick attack.

TREMOLO PICKING: The note is picked as rapidly and continuously as possible.

VIBRATO BAR DIVE AND RETURN: The pitch of the note or chord is dropped a specified number of steps (in rhythm), then returned to the original pitch.

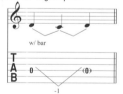

VIBRATO BAR SCOOP: Depress the bar just before striking the note, then quickly release the bar.

VIBRATO BAR DIP: Strike the note and then immediately drop a specified number of steps, then release back to the original pitch.

Additional Musical Definitions

(accent)   • Accentuate note (play it louder).

(staccato)   • Play the note short.

D.S. al Coda   • Go back to the sign (§), then play until the measure marked "*To Coda*," then skip to the section labelled "*Coda*."

D.C. al Fine   • Go back to the beginning of the song and play until the measure marked "*Fine*" (end).

Fill   • Label used to identify a brief melodic figure which is to be inserted into the arrangement.

N.C.   • Harmony is implied.

• Repeat measures between signs.

• When a repeated section has different endings, play the first ending only the first time and the second ending only the second time.

Europa

Words and Music by Carlos Santana and Tom Coster

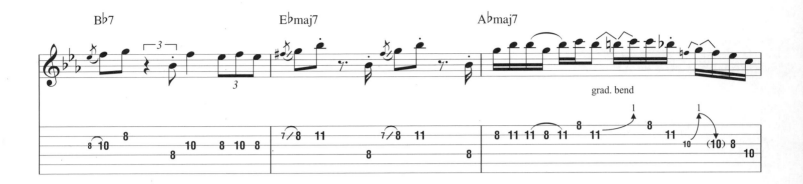

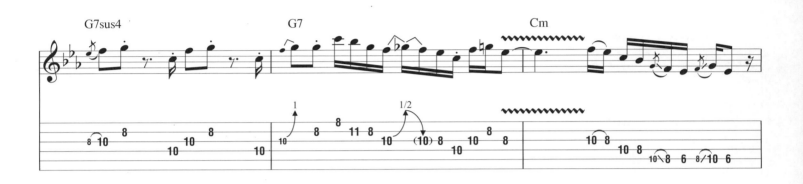

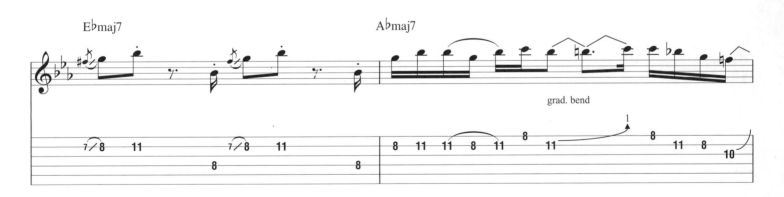

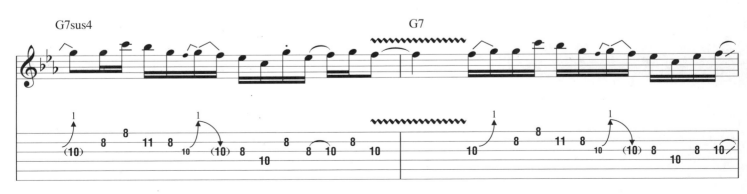

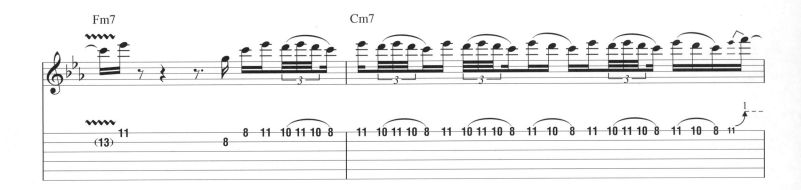

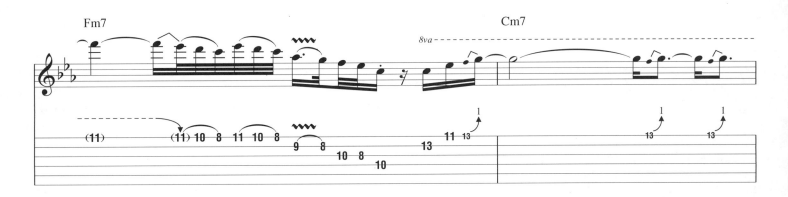

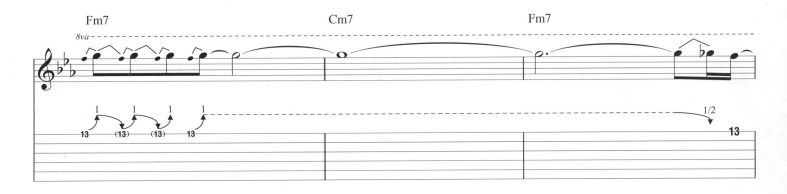

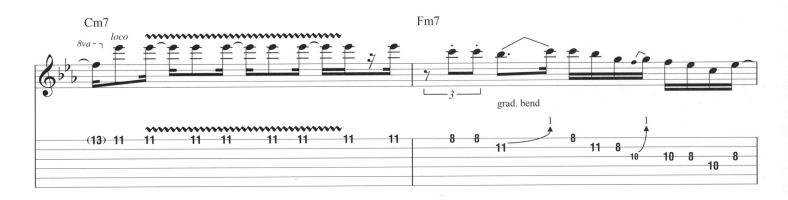

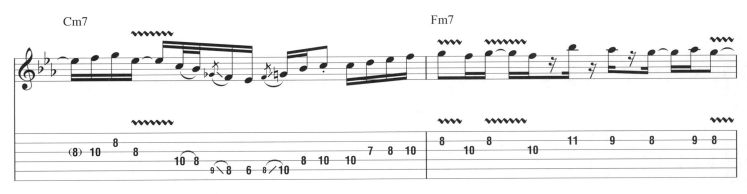

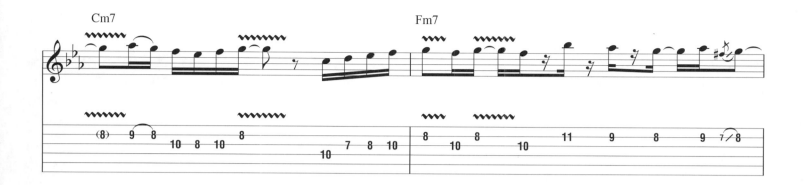

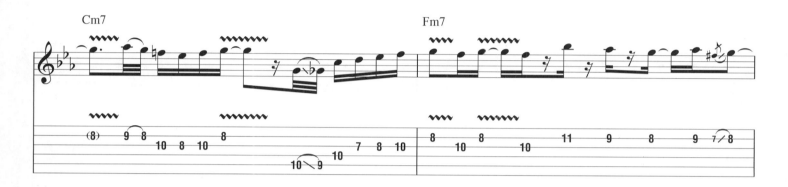

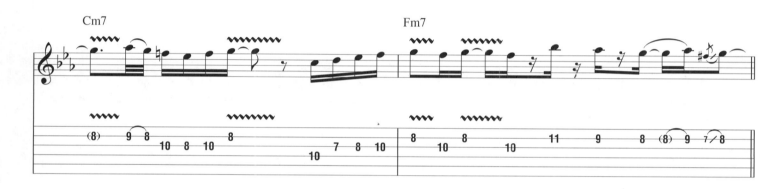

F

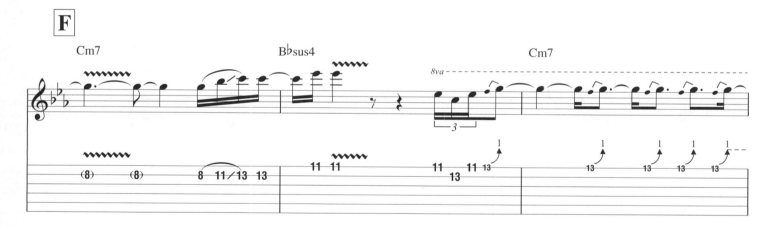

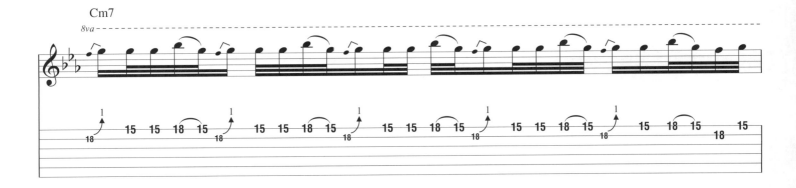

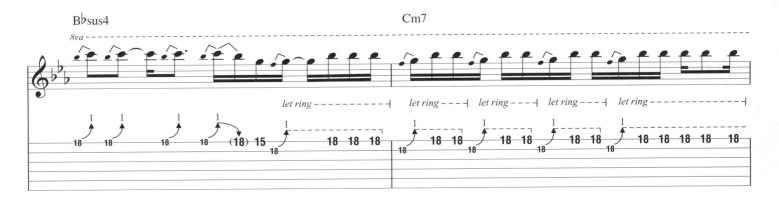

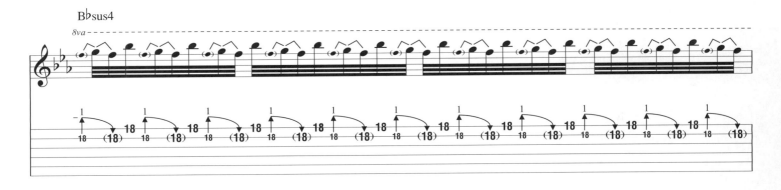

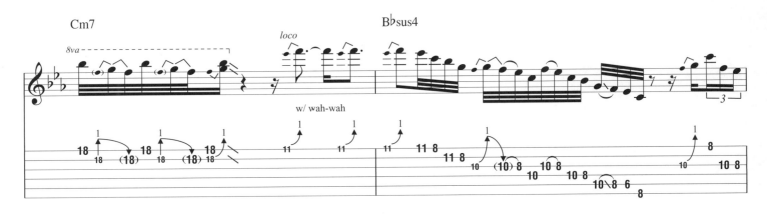

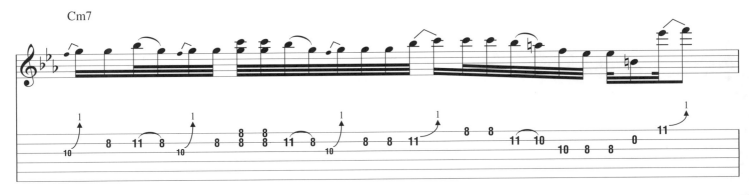

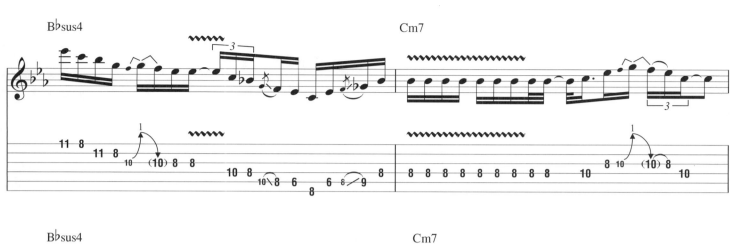

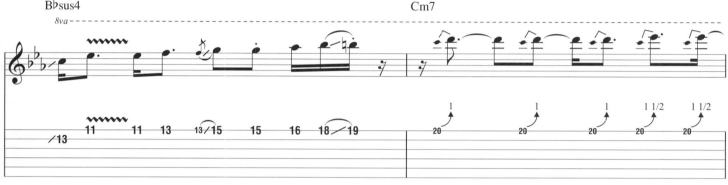

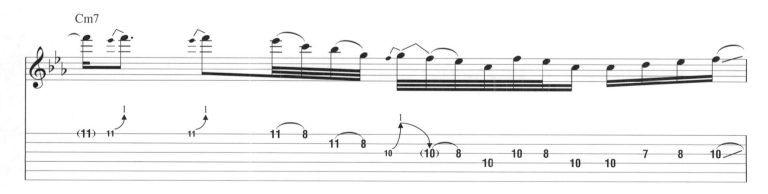

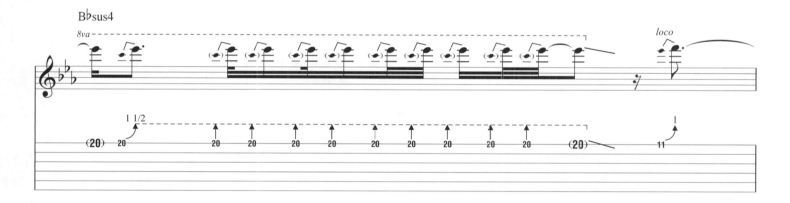

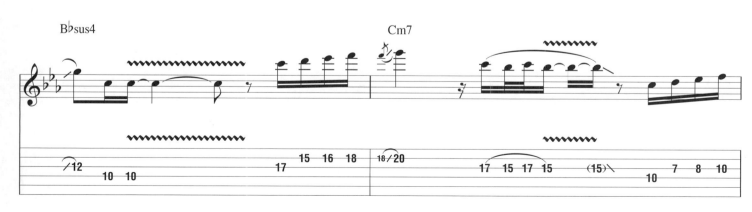

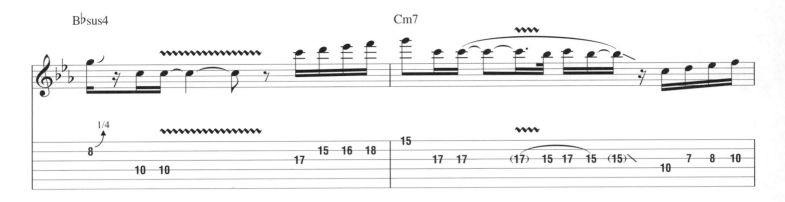

Begin fade

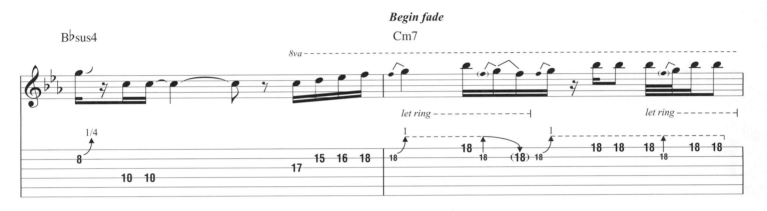

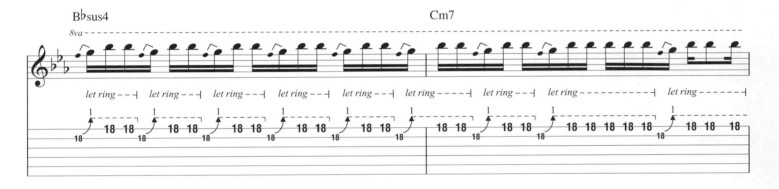

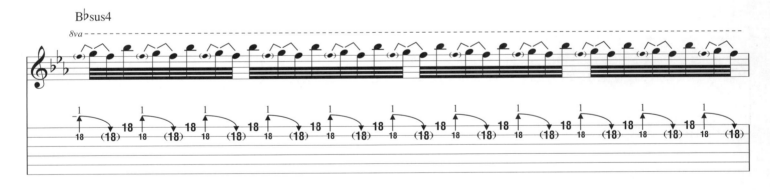

Fade out

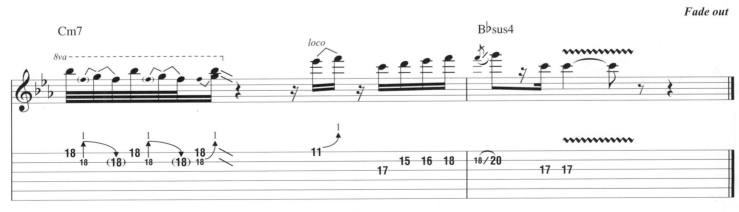

14

Everything's Coming Our Way

Words and Music by Carlos Santana

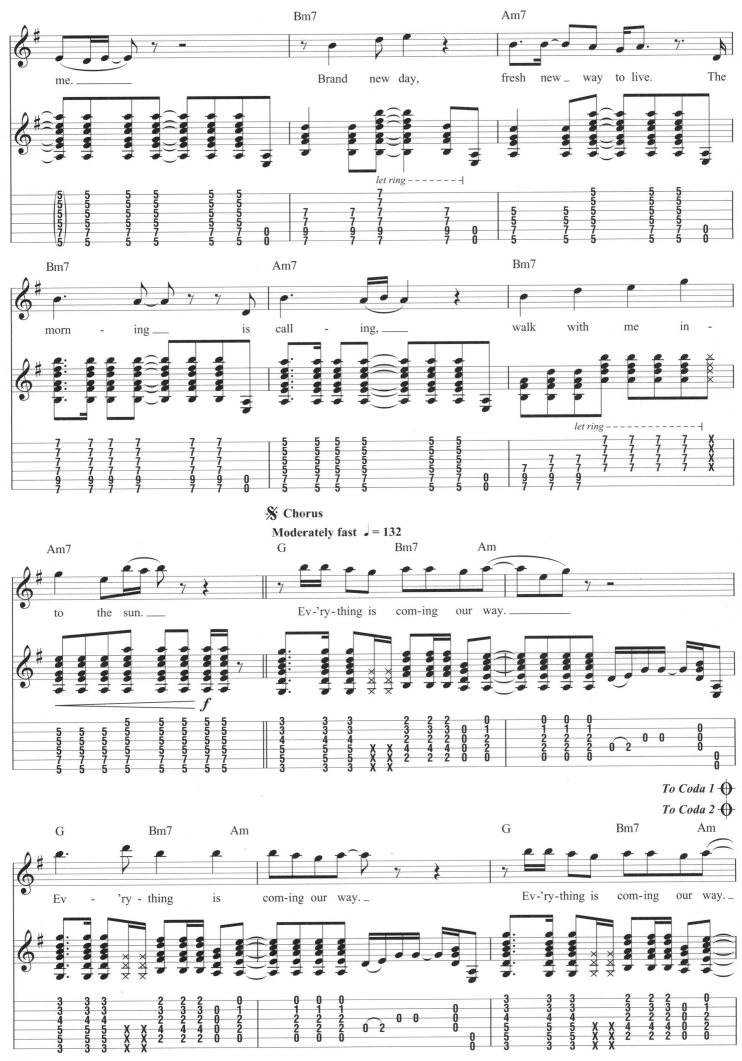

§ **Chorus**

Moderately fast ♩ = 132

To Coda 1 ⊕
To Coda 2 ⊕

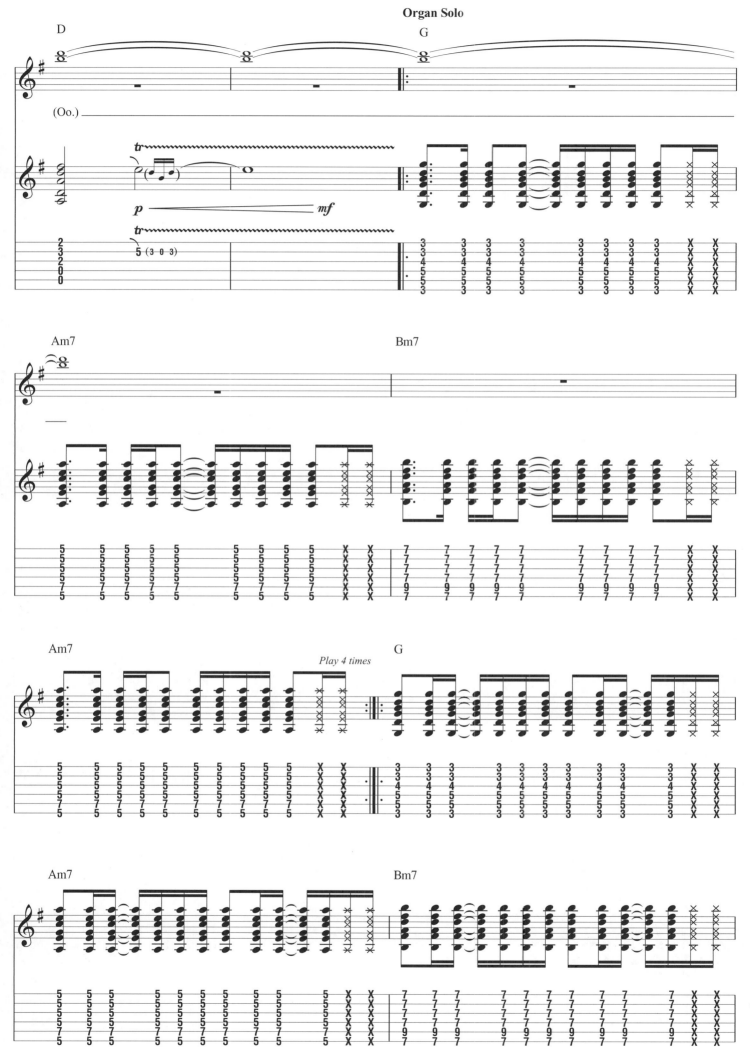

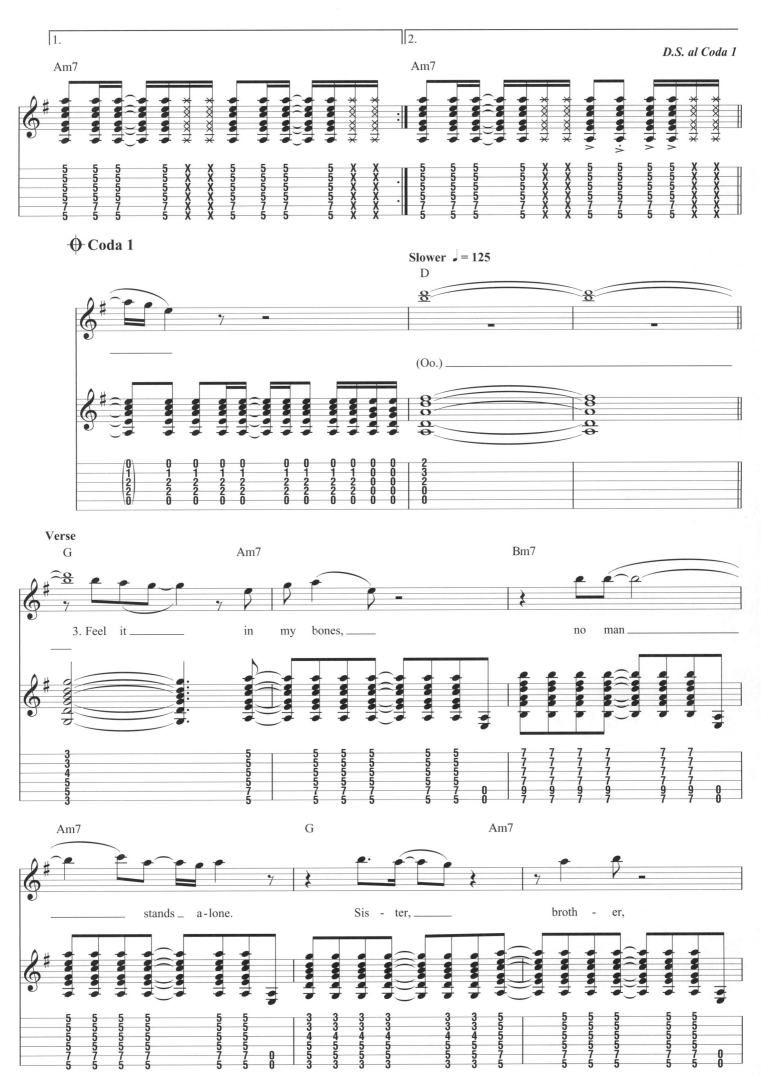

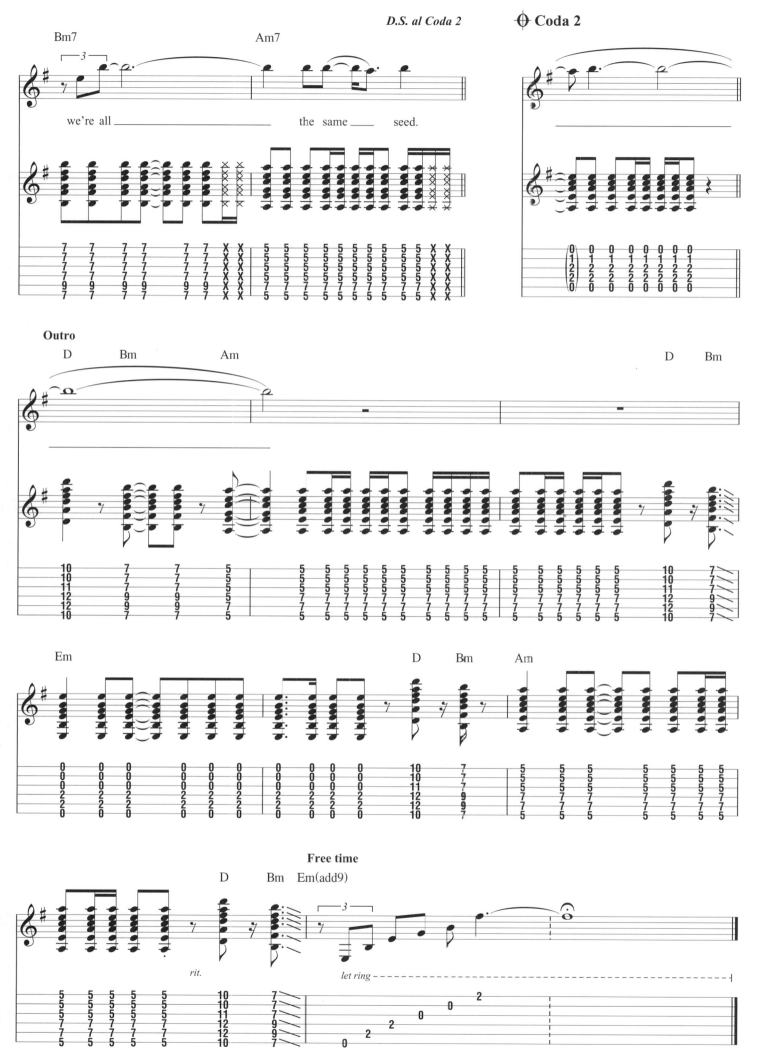

No One to Depend On

Words and Music by Gregg Rolie, Michael Carabello and Thomas Escovedo

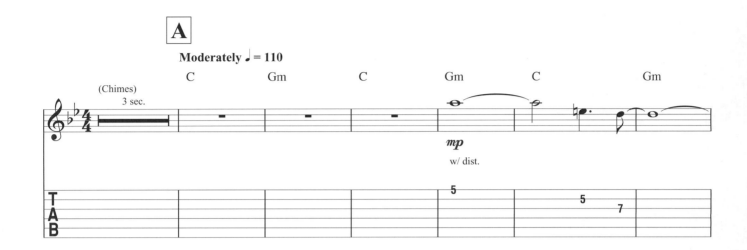

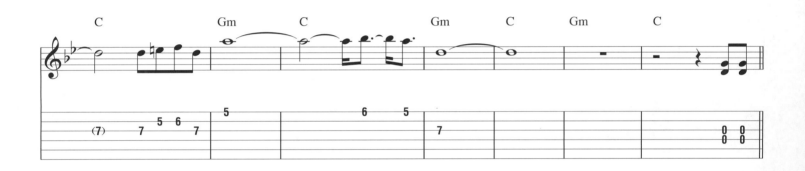

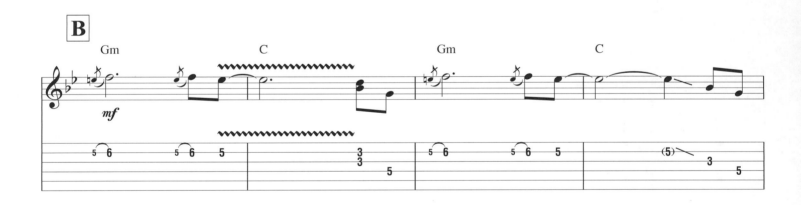

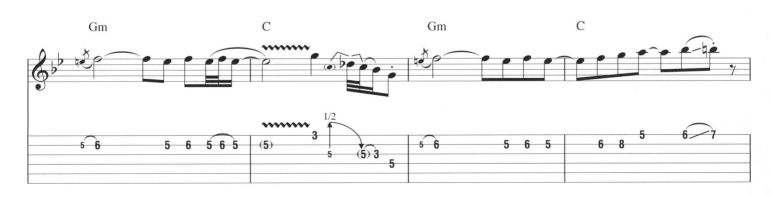

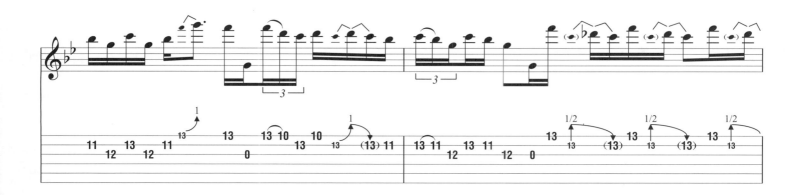

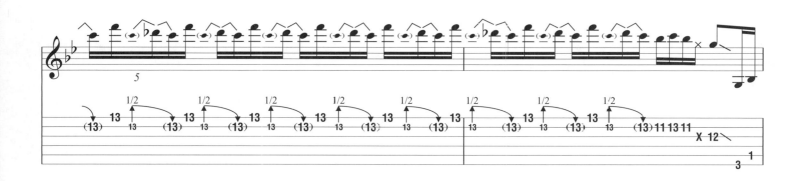

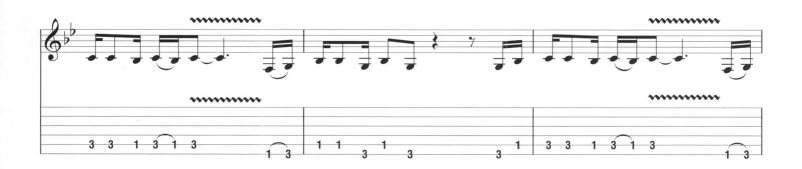

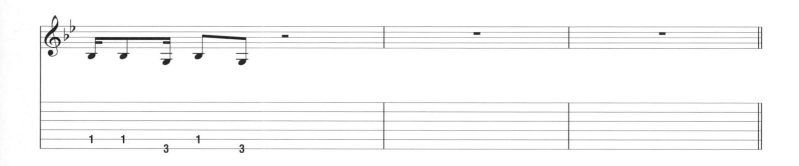

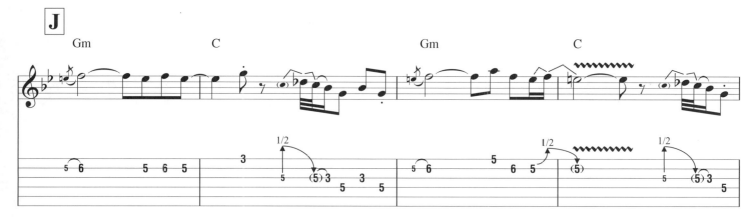

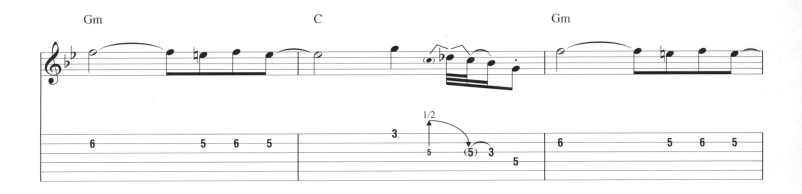

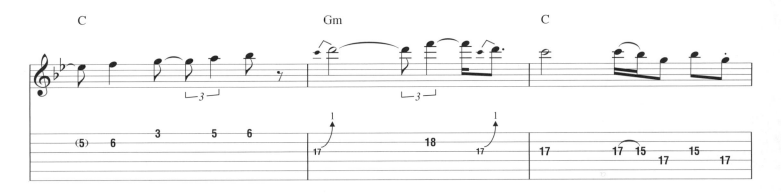

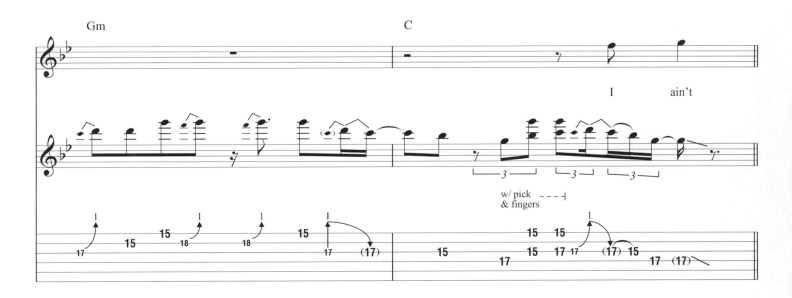

K

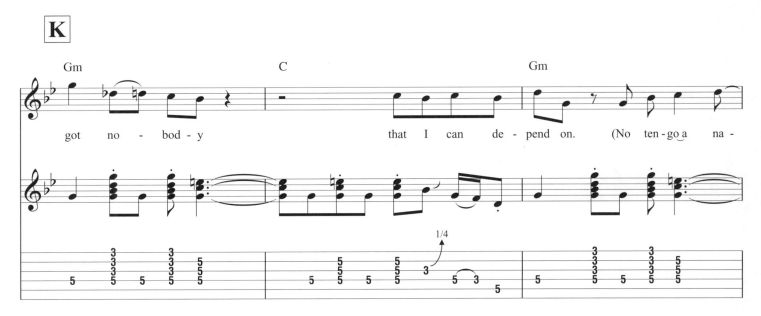

got no - bod - y   that I can de - pend on. (No ten - go a na -

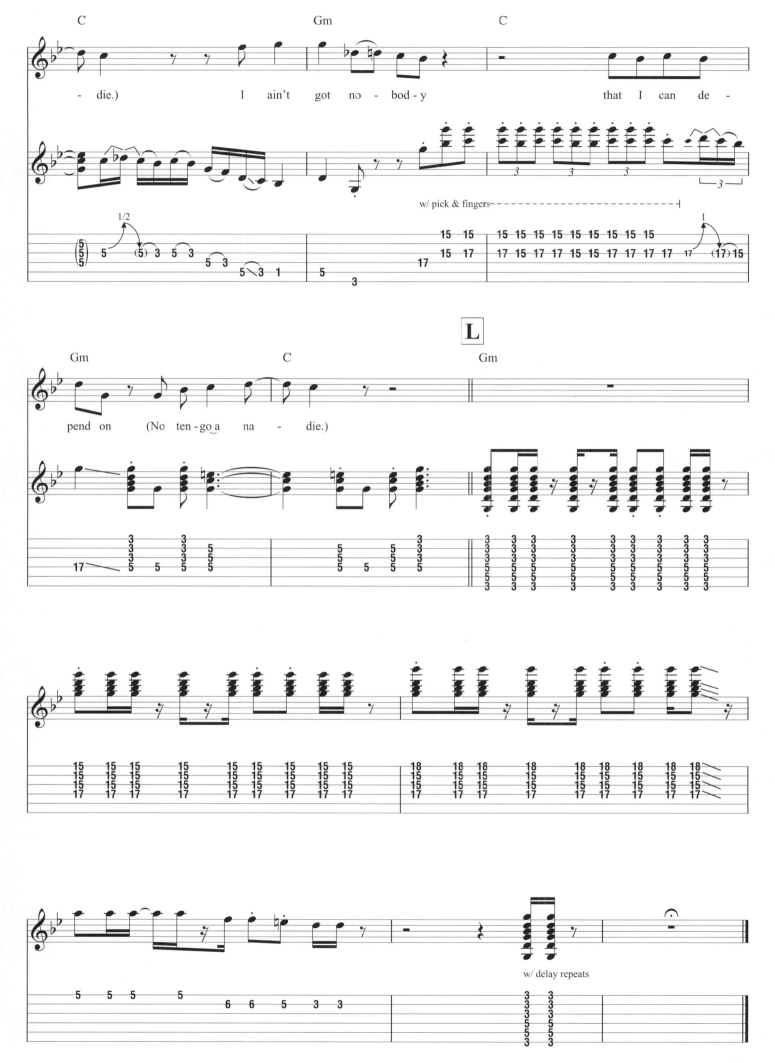

Smooth

Words by Rob Thomas
Music by Rob Thomas and Itaal Shur

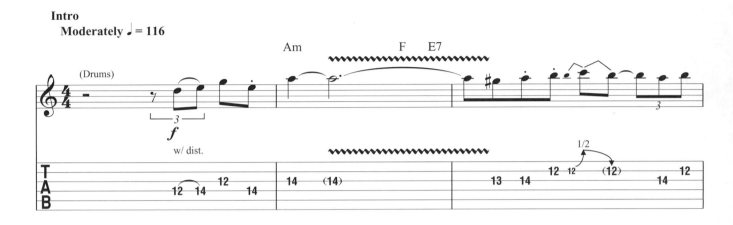

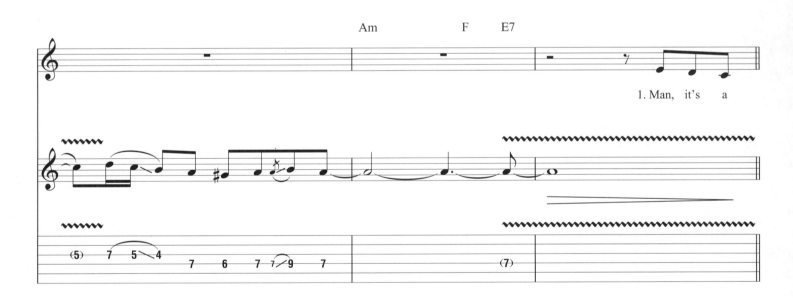

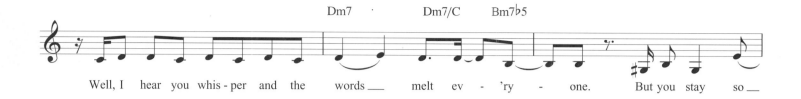

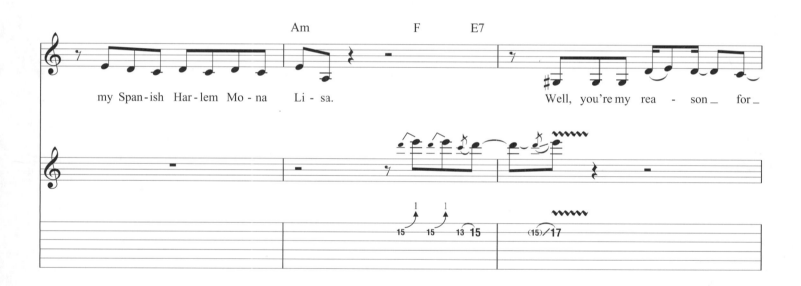

Pre-Chorus

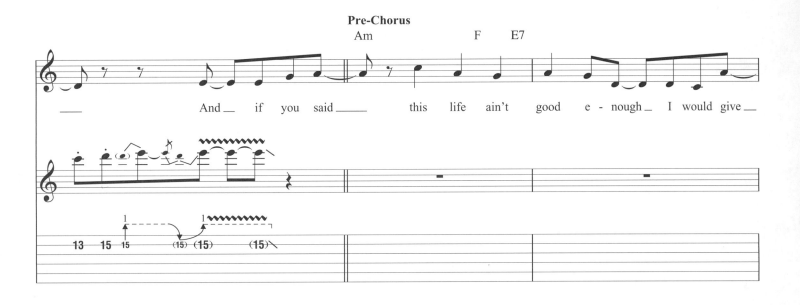

And__ if you said____ this life ain't good e-nough__ I would give__

____ my world to lift you up.___ I could change__ my life to

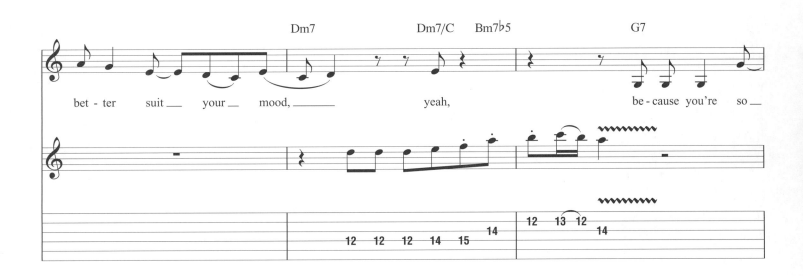

bet-ter suit__ your__ mood,____ yeah, be-cause you're so__

Chorus

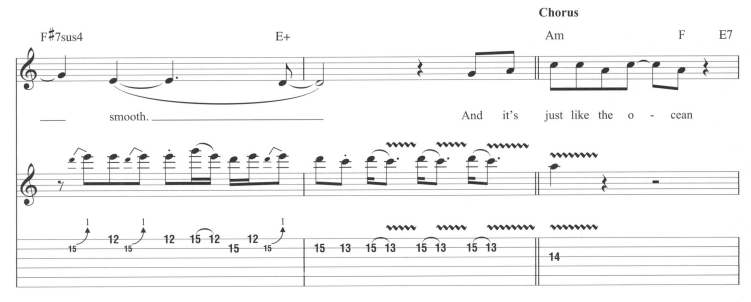

____ smooth._____ And it's just like the o-cean

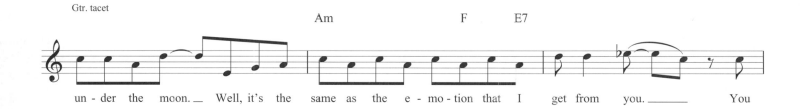

Gtr. tacet

un-der the moon. _ Well, it's the same as the e - mo - tion that I get from you. _____ You

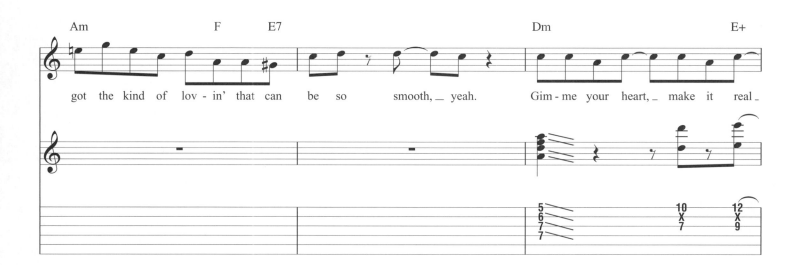

got the kind of lov - in' that can be so smooth, _ yeah. Gim - me your heart, _ make it real _

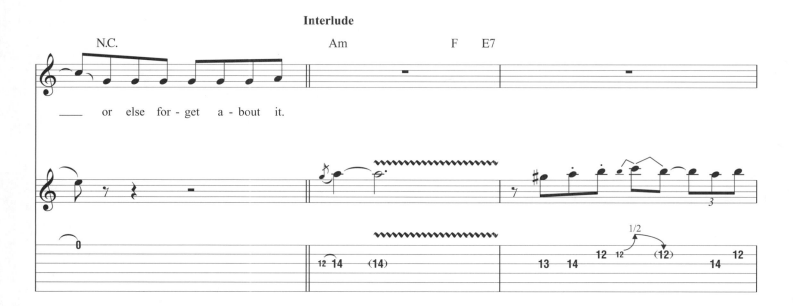

Interlude

_____ or else for - get a - bout it.

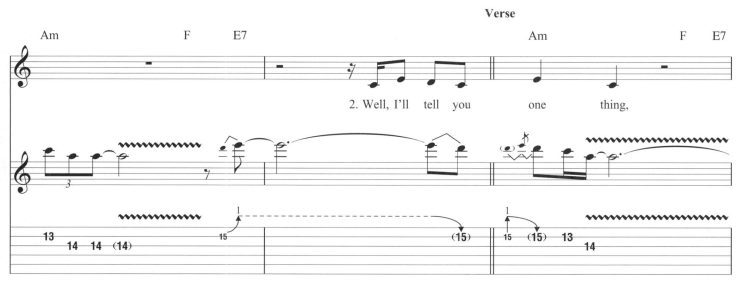

Verse

2. Well, I'll tell you one thing,

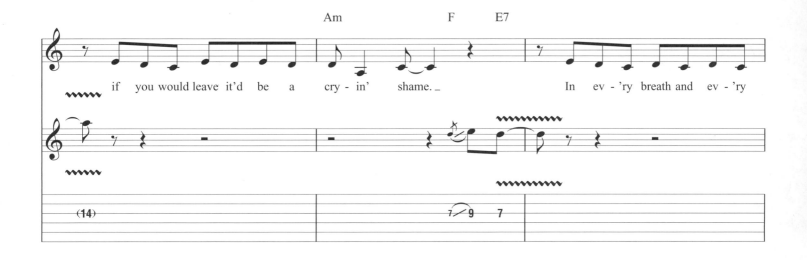

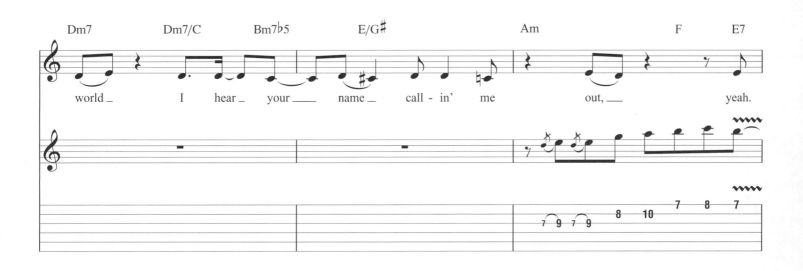

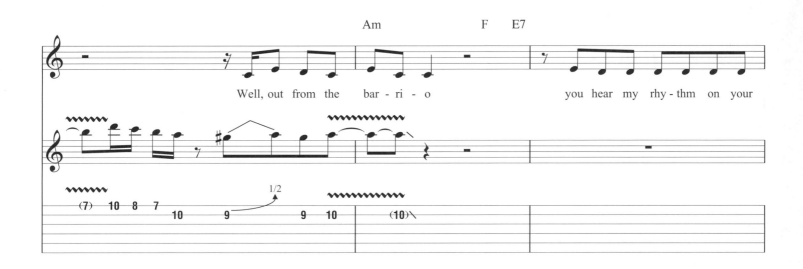

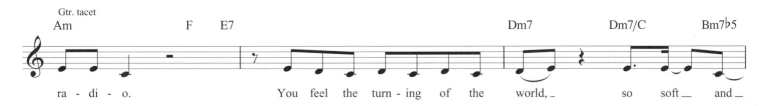

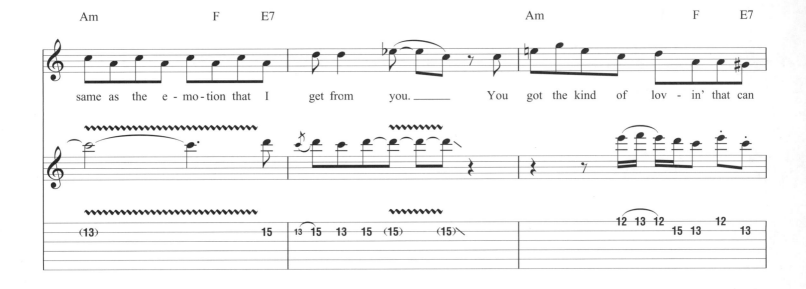

same as the e-mo-tion that I get from you.____ You got the kind of lov-in' that can

be so smooth, yeah. Gim-mie your heart,_ make it real,___ or else for-get a-bout it.

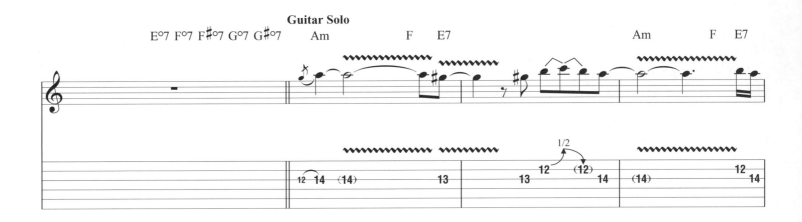

Guitar Solo

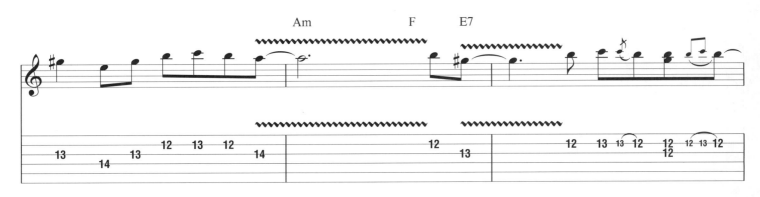

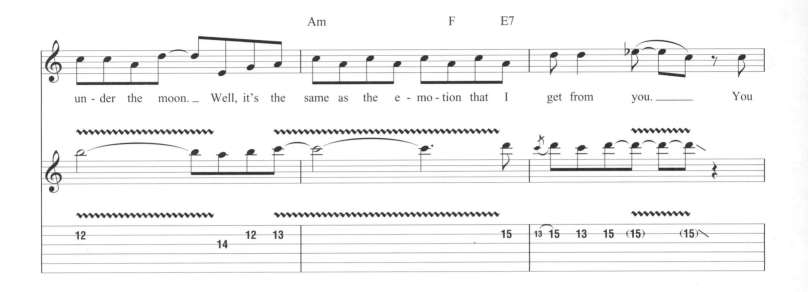

Am   F   E7

un - der the moon. _ Well, it's the same as the e - mo - tion that I get from you. _____ You

Am   F   E7   Dm7   E+

got the kind of lov - in' that can be so smooth, _ yeah. Gim - me your heart, _ make it real,

Outro-Guitar Solo

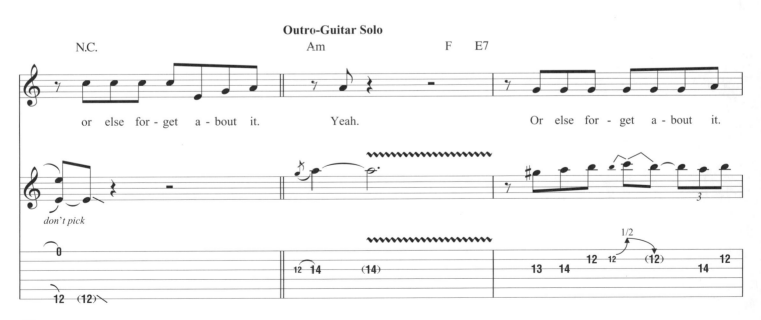

N.C.   Am   F   E7

or else for - get a - bout it. Yeah. Or else for - get a - bout it.

don't pick

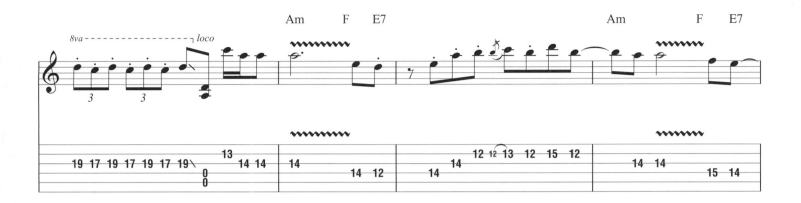

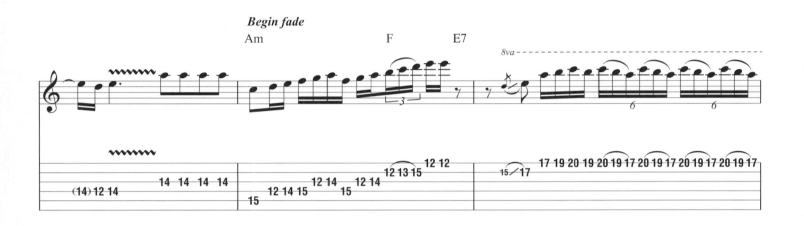

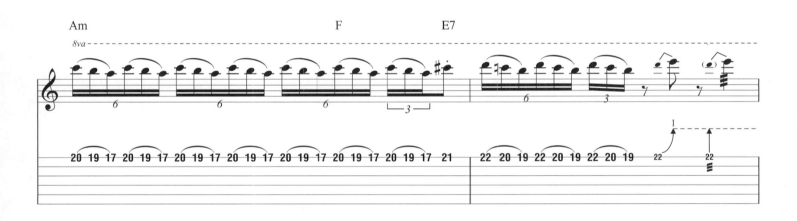

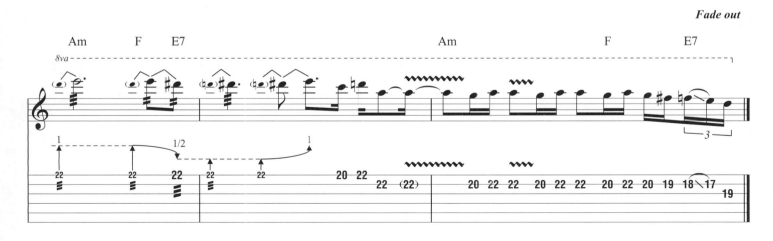

Evil Ways

Words and Music by Sonny Henry

Intro
Moderately ♩ = 118

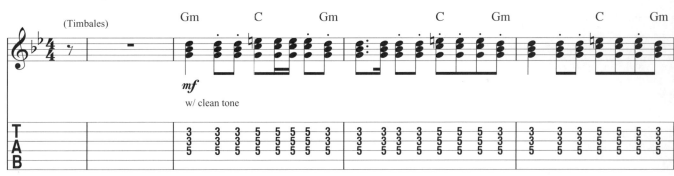

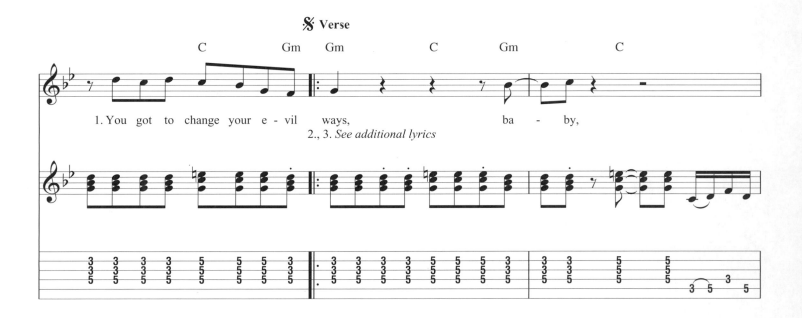

1. You got to change your e-vil ways, ba - by,
2., 3. *See additional lyrics*

be - fore I start lov - in' you.__ You got to change,__ ba -

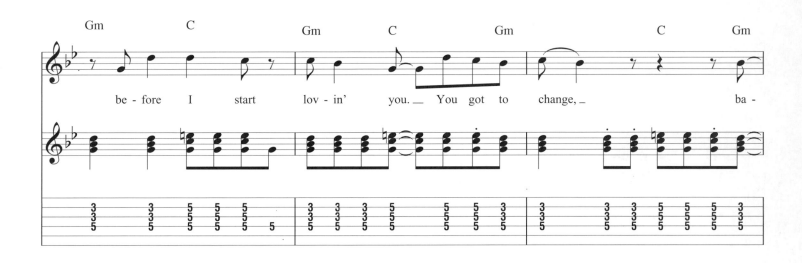

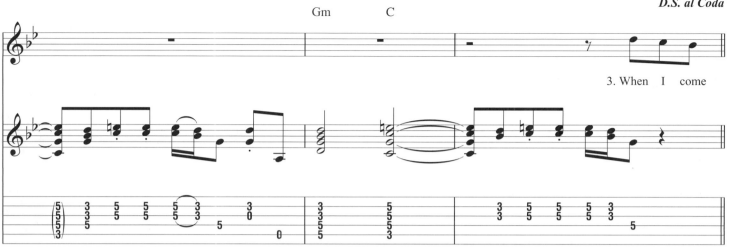

Gm   C

3. When I come

Coda

D7   N.C.   Gm   C7

on,   yeah,   yeah,   yeah!

f
w/ dist.

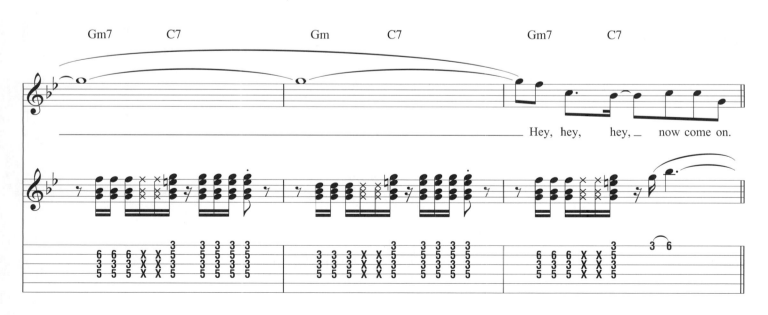

Gm7   C7   Gm   C7   Gm7   C7

Hey, hey, hey,___ now come on.

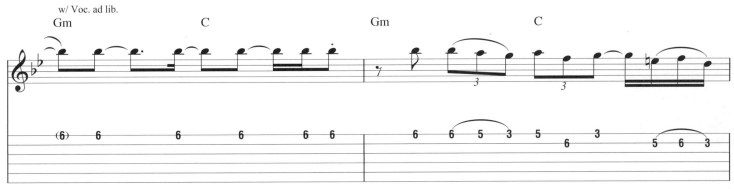

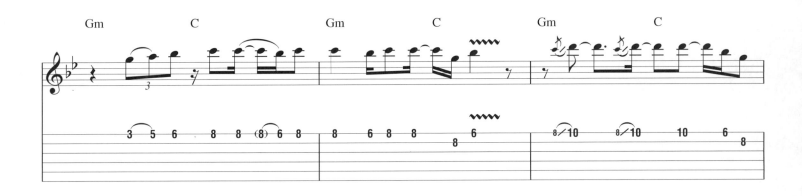

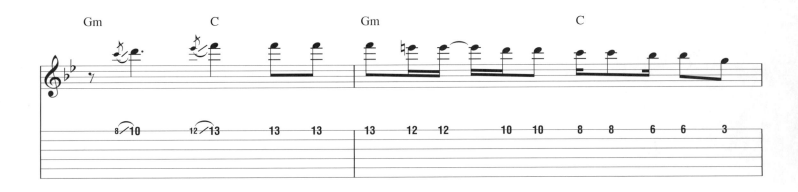

Fade out

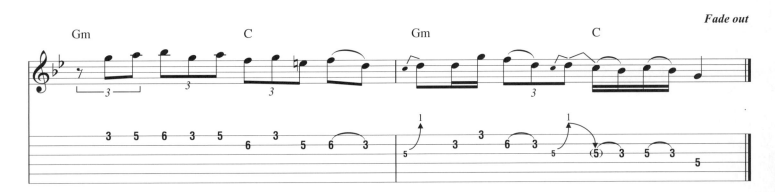

Additional Lyrics

2., 3. When I come home, baby,
My house is dark and my pots are cold.
You hangin' 'round, baby,
With Jean and Joan and a who knows who.
I'm gettin' tired of waitin' and fooling around.
I'll find somebody that won't make me feel like a clown.
This can't go on...

Oye Como Va

Words and Music by Tito Puente

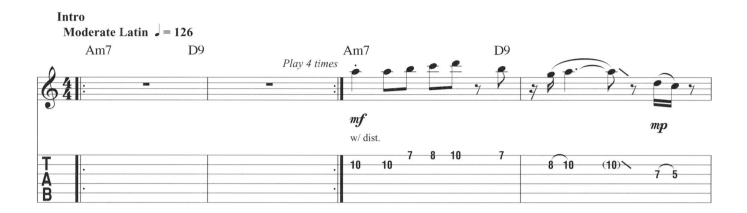

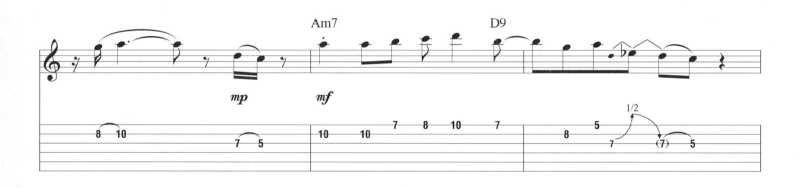

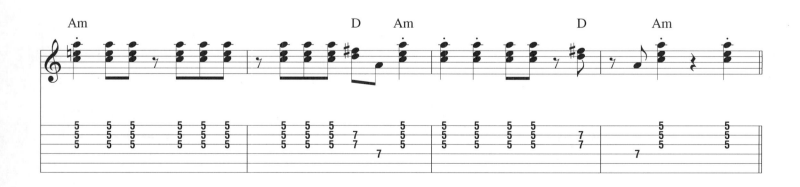

Verse

1. Oy - e co - mo va, mi rit - mo. Bue - no pa go - zar, mu - la - ta.

Oy - e co - mo va, mi rit - mo. Bue - no pa go - zar, mu - la - ta.

Guitar Solo

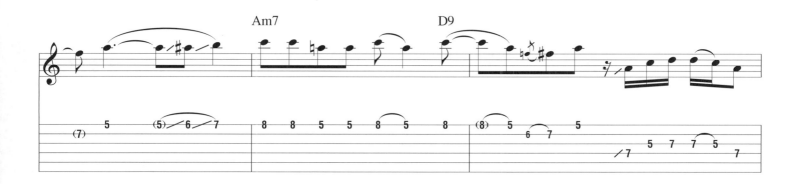

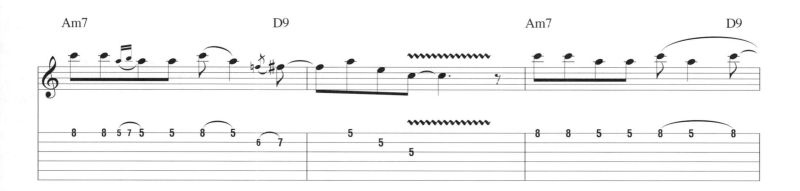

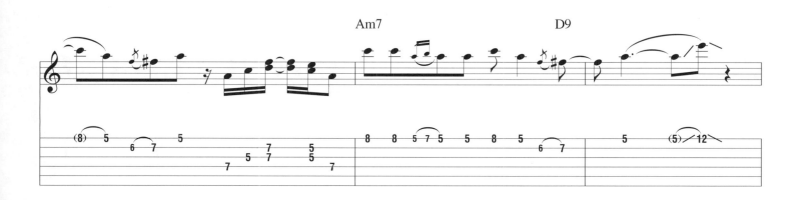

Interlude

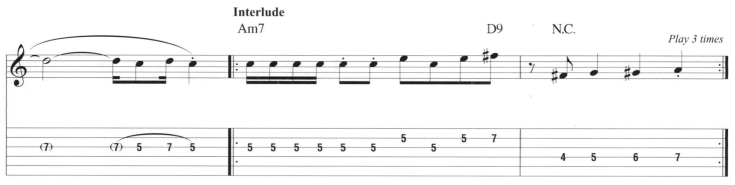

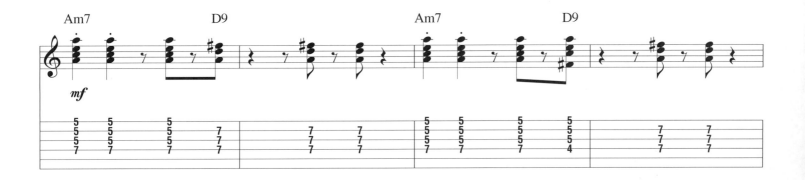

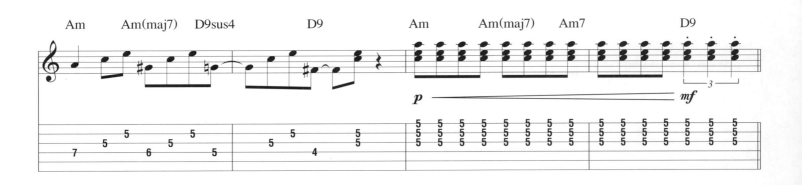

Organ Solo

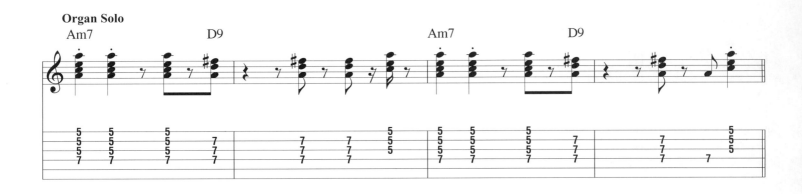

Play 4 times

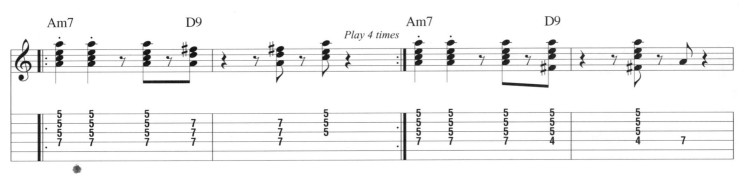

Bridge

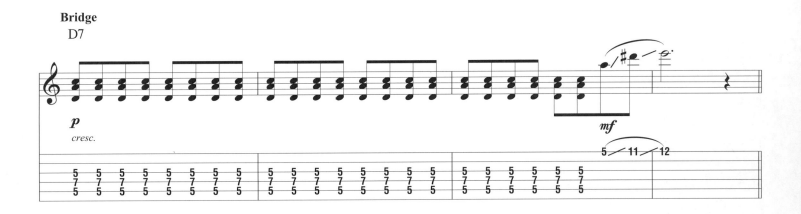

Guitar Solo

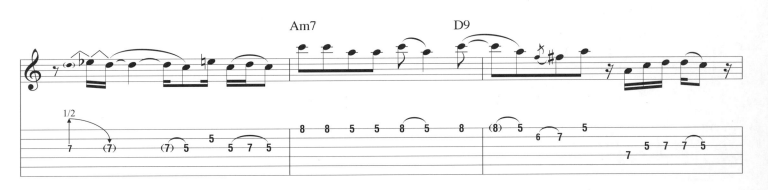

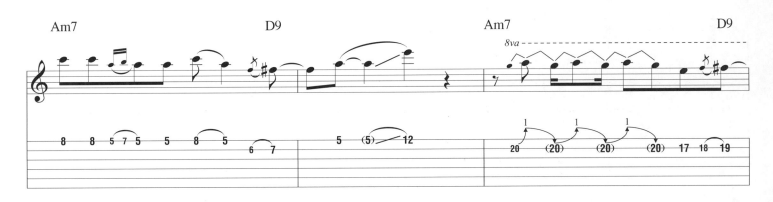

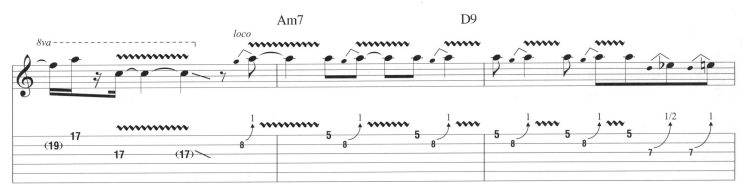

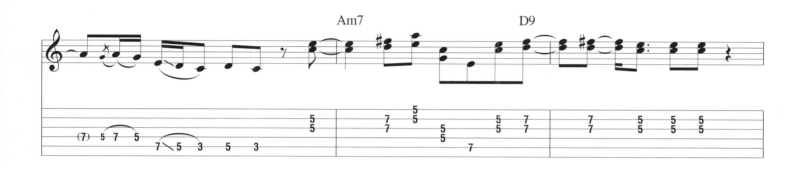

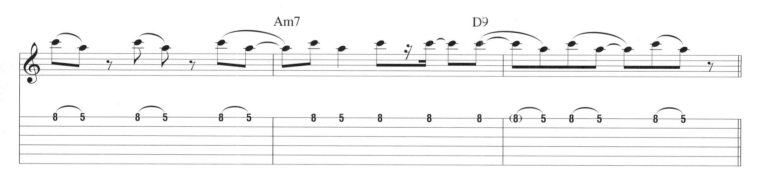

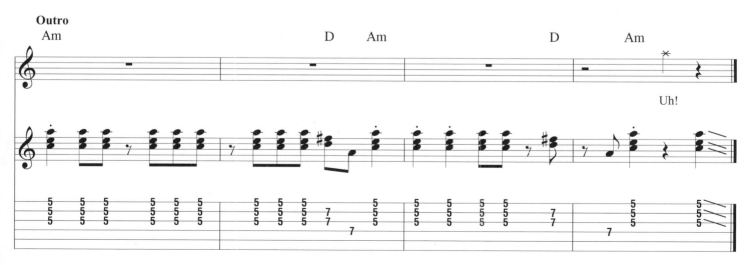

Samba Pa Ti

Words and Music by Carlos Santana

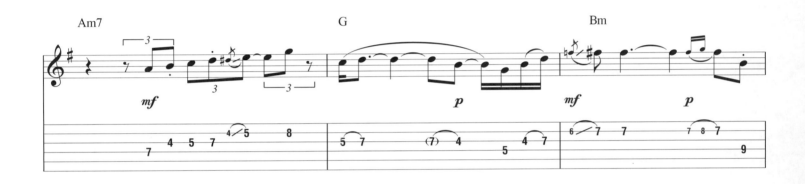

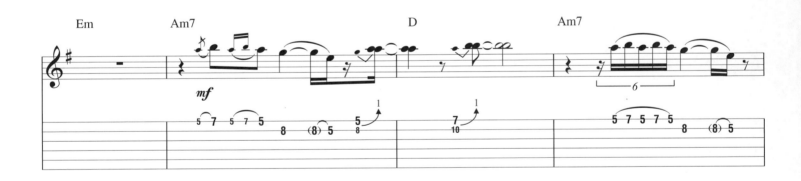

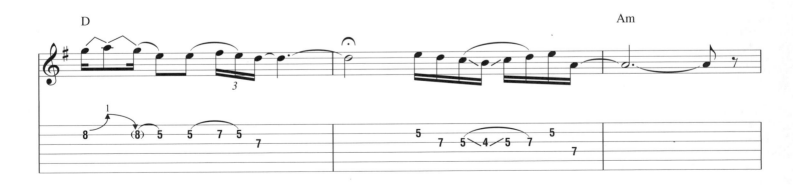

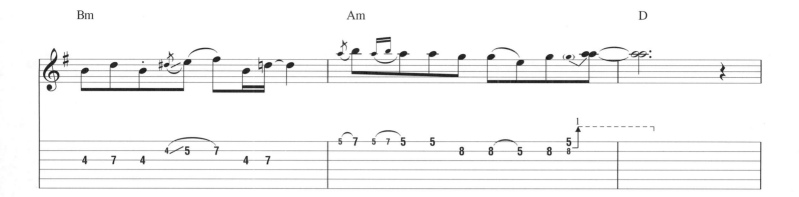

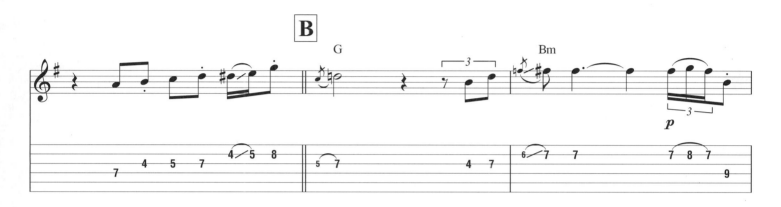

B

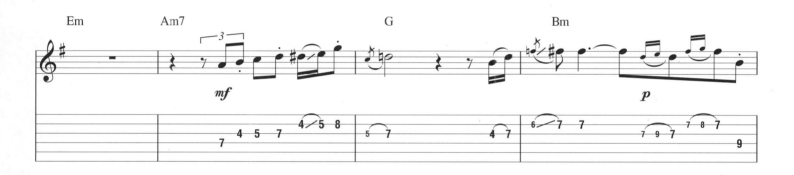

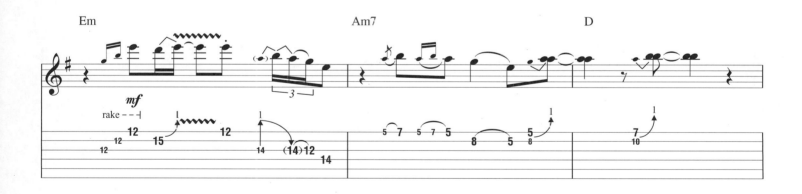

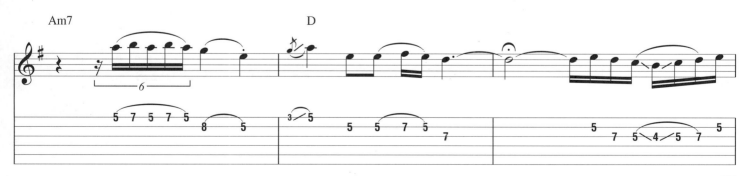

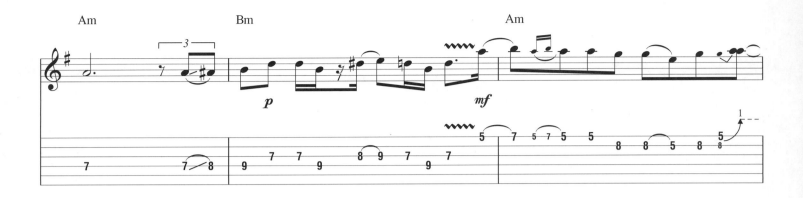

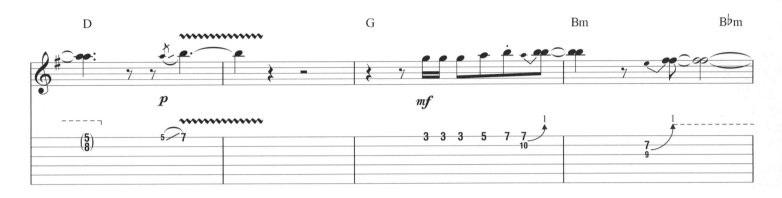

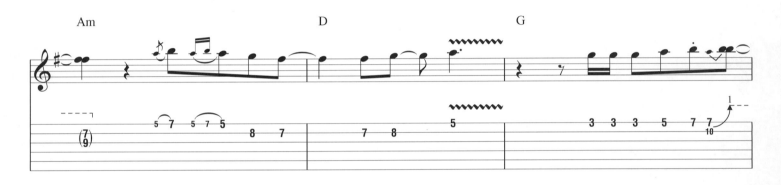

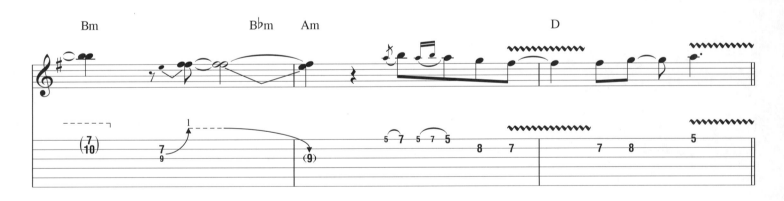

C

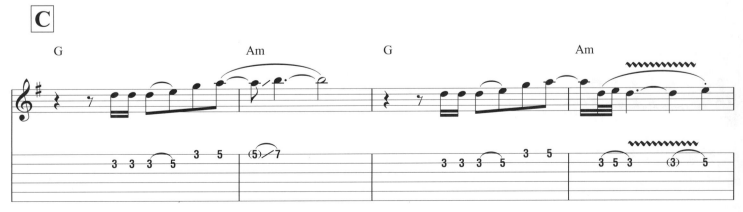

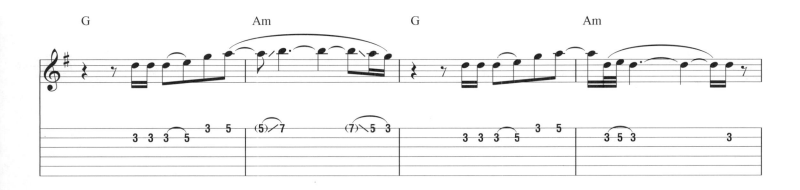

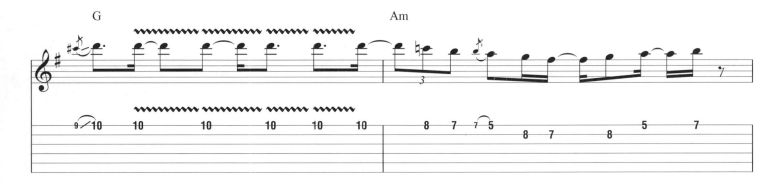

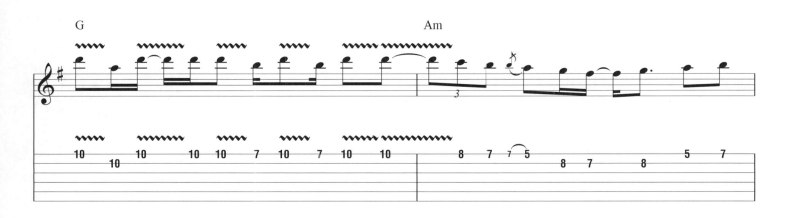

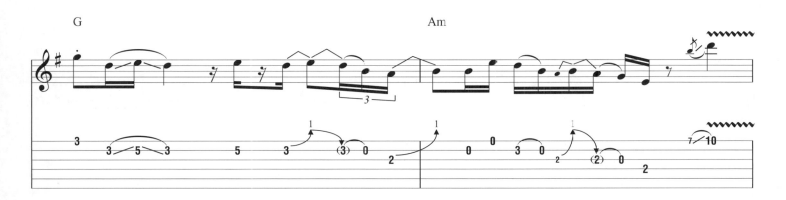

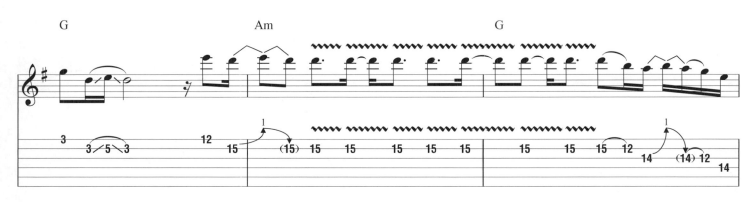

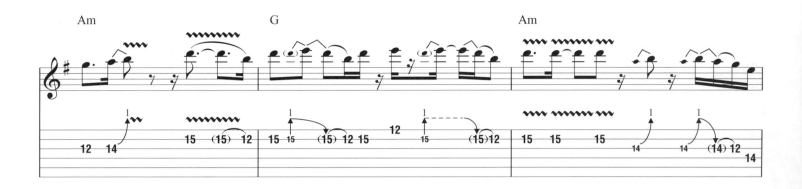

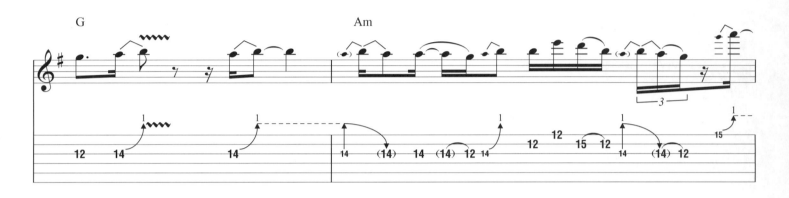

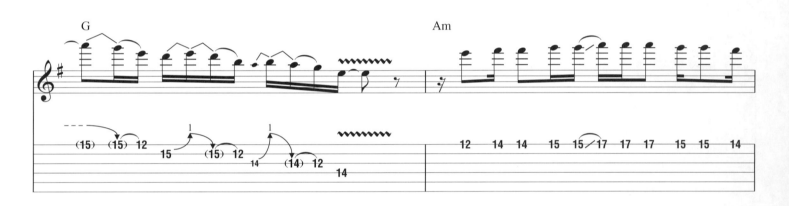

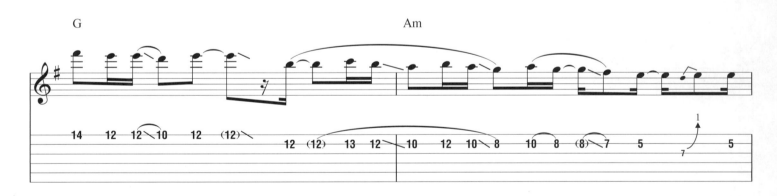

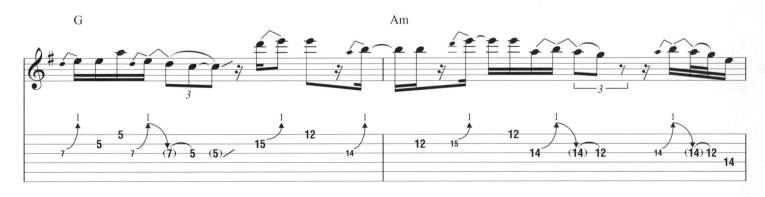

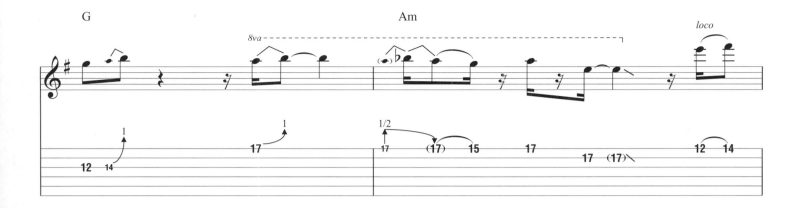

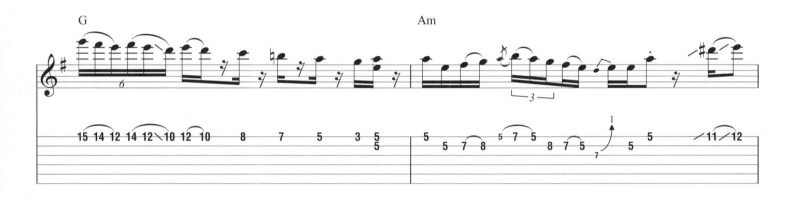

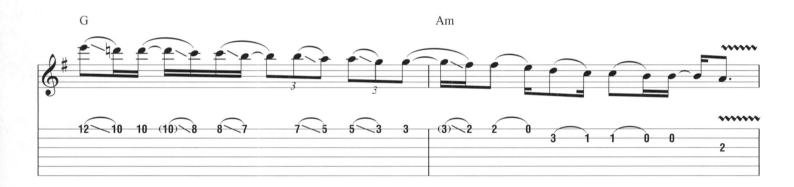

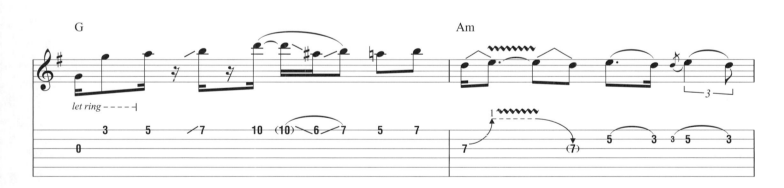

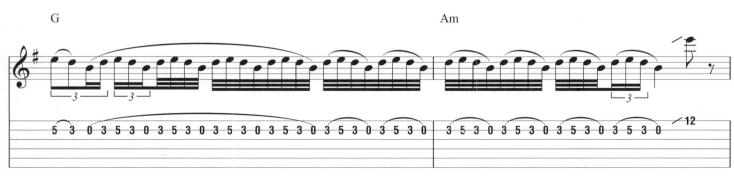

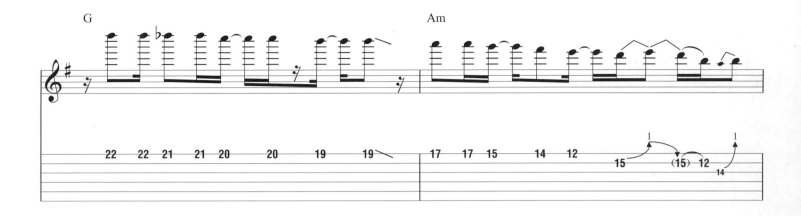

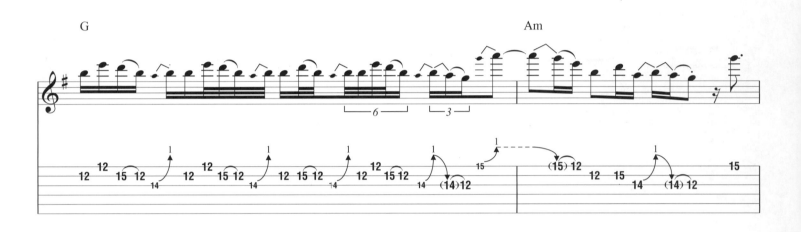

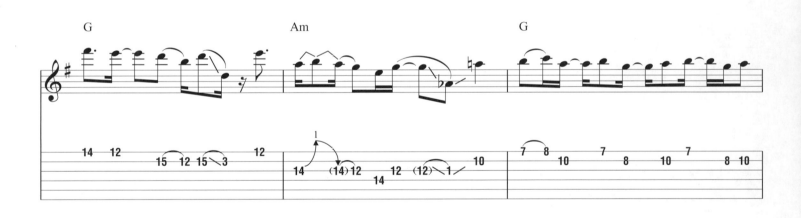

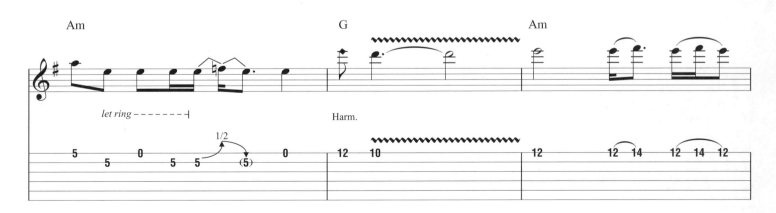

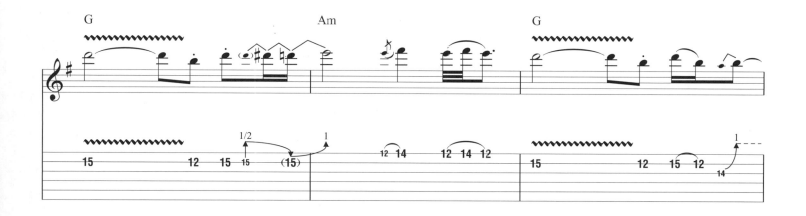

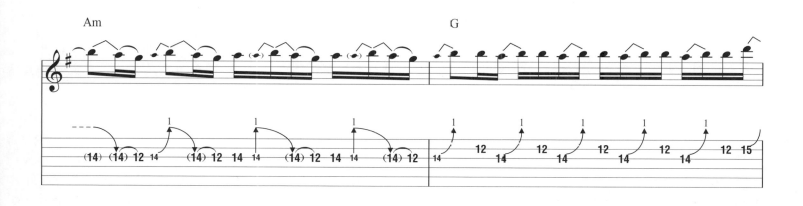

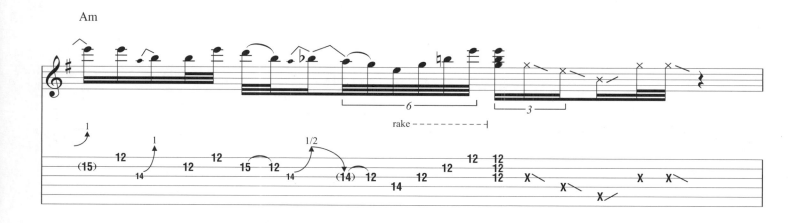

Soul Sacrifice

By Carlos Santana

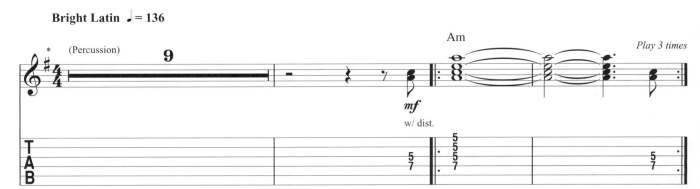

*Key signature denotes A Dorian.

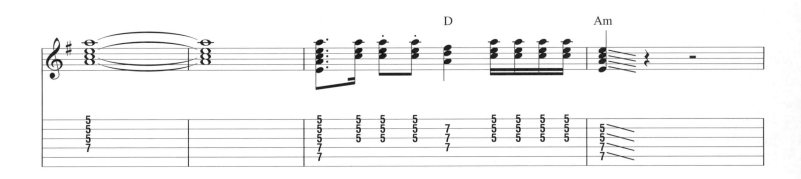

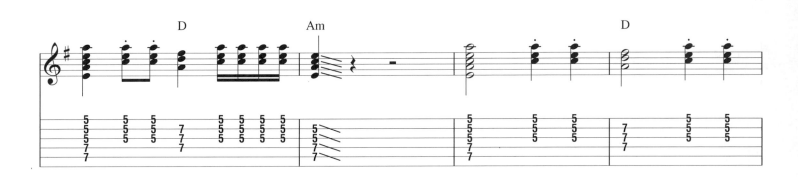

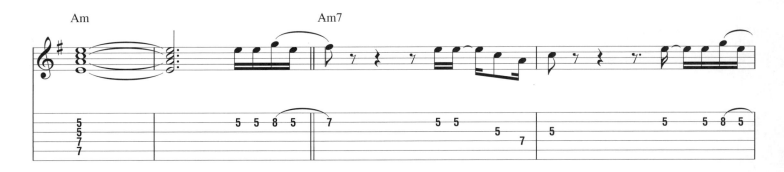

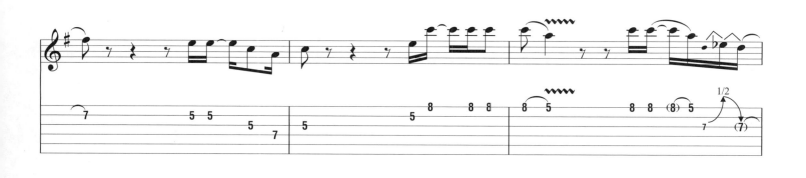

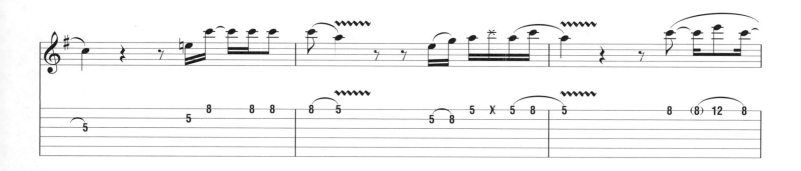

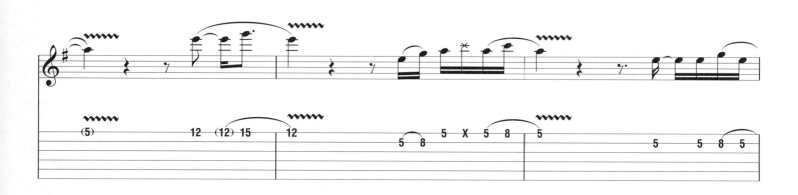

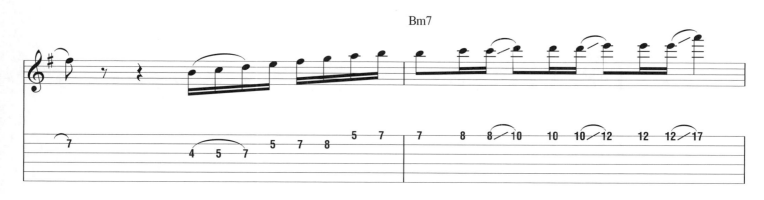

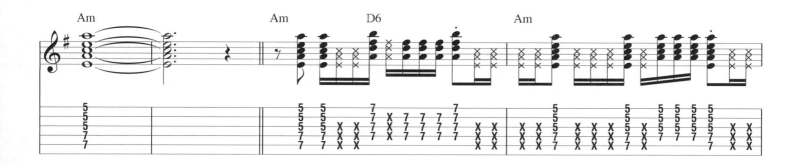

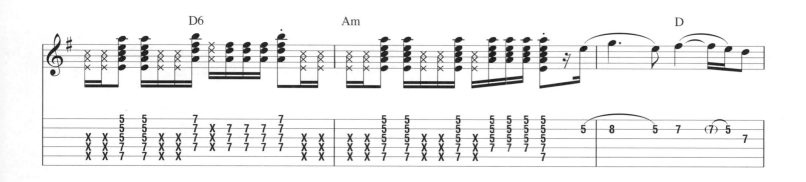

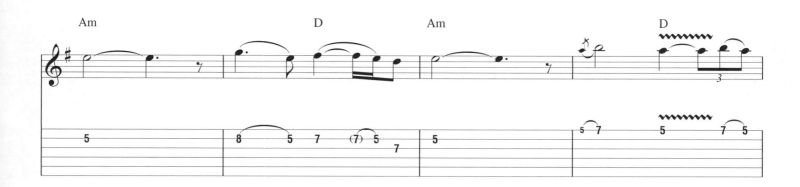

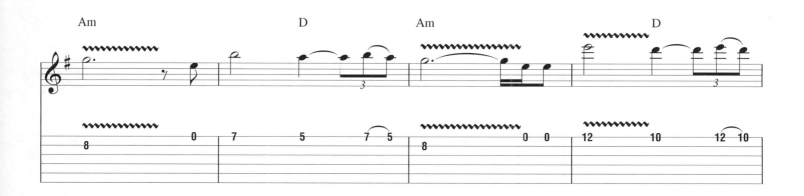

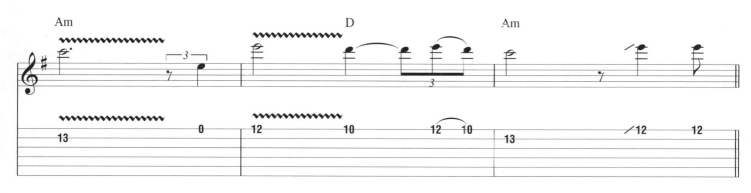

Guitar Solo

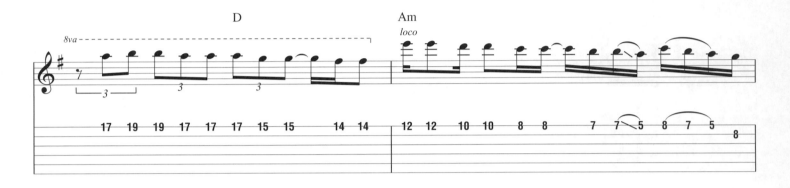

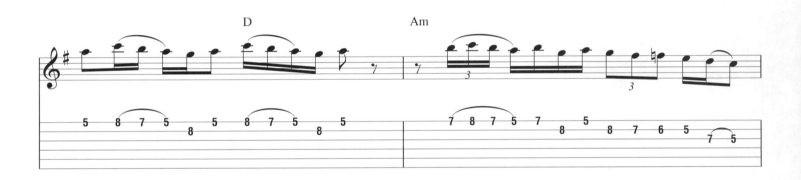

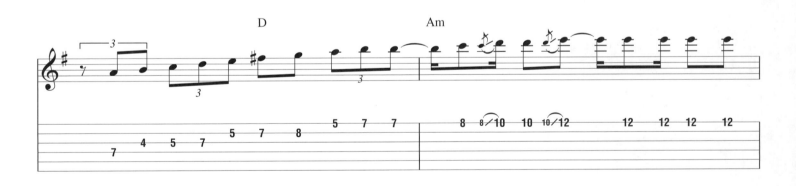

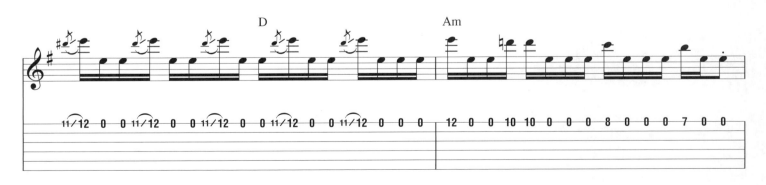

Organ Solo

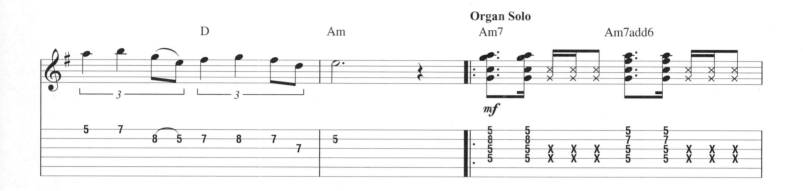

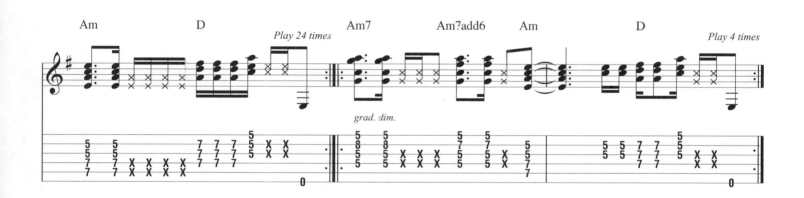

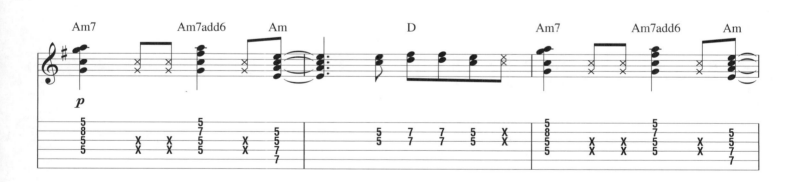

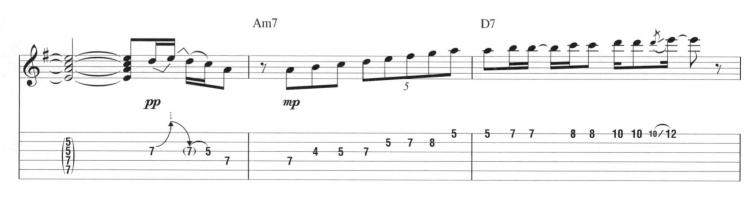

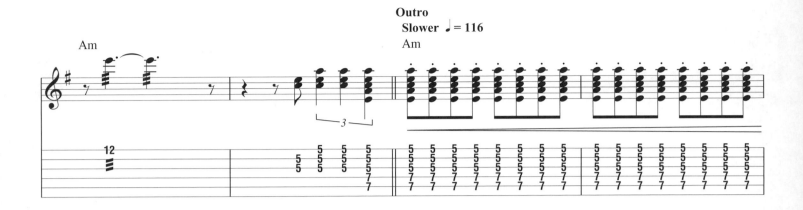

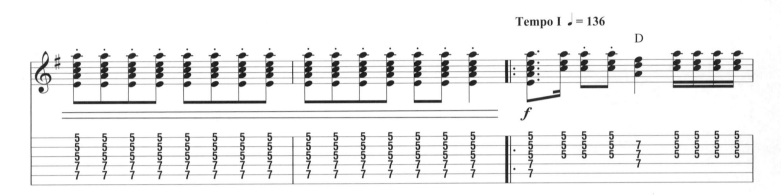

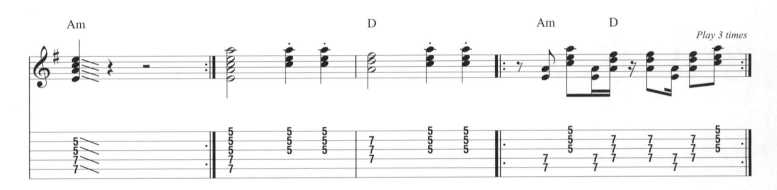

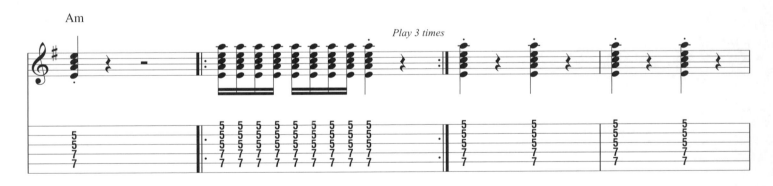

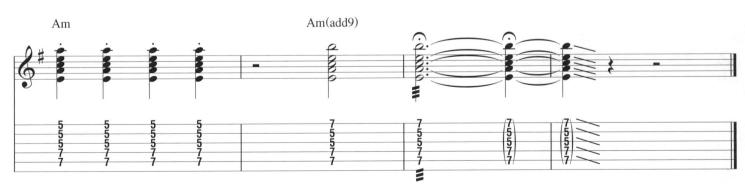

HAL•LEONARD® GUITAR PLAY-ALONG

INCLUDES TAB

AUDIO ACCESS INCLUDED

This series will help you play your favorite songs quickly and easily. Just follow the tab and listen to the audio to hear how the guitar should sound, and then play along using the separate backing tracks.

Playback tools are provided for slowing down the tempo without changing pitch and looping challenging parts. The melody and lyrics are included in the book so that you can sing or simply follow along.

107. CREAM
00701069...................$17.99

108. THE WHO
00701053...................$17.99

109. STEVE MILLER
00701054...................$19.99

110. SLIDE GUITAR HITS
00701055...................$17.99

111. JOHN MELLENCAMP
00701056...................$14.99

112. QUEEN
00701052...................$16.99

113. JIM CROCE
00701058...................$19.99

114. BON JOVI
00701060...................$17.99

115. JOHNNY CASH
00701070...................$17.99

116. THE VENTURES
00701124...................$17.99

117. BRAD PAISLEY
00701224...................$16.99

118. ERIC JOHNSON
00701353...................$17.99

119. AC/DC CLASSICS
00701356...................$19.99

120. PROGRESSIVE ROCK
00701457...................$14.99

121. U2
00701508...................$17.99

122. CROSBY, STILLS & NASH
00701610...................$16.99

123. LENNON & McCARTNEY ACOUSTIC
00701614...................$16.99

124. SMOOTH JAZZ
00200664...................$16.99

125. JEFF BECK
00701687...................$19.99

126. BOB MARLEY
00701701...................$17.99

127. 1970S ROCK
00701739...................$17.99

128. 1960S ROCK
00701740...................$14.99

129. MEGADETH
00701741...................$17.99

130. IRON MAIDEN
00701742...................$17.99

131. 1990S ROCK
00701743...................$14.99

132. COUNTRY ROCK
00701757...................$15.99

133. TAYLOR SWIFT
00701894...................$16.99

135. MINOR BLUES
00151350...................$17.99

136. GUITAR THEMES
00701922...................$14.99

137. IRISH TUNES
00701966...................$15.99

138. BLUEGRASS CLASSICS
00701967...................$17.99

139. GARY MOORE
00702370...................$17.99

140. MORE STEVIE RAY VAUGHAN
00702396...................$19.99

141. ACOUSTIC HITS
00702401...................$16.99

142. GEORGE HARRISON
00237697...................$17.99

143. SLASH
00702425...................$19.99

144. DJANGO REINHARDT
00702531...................$17.99

145. DEF LEPPARD
00702532...................$19.99

146. ROBERT JOHNSON
00702533...................$16.99

147. SIMON & GARFUNKEL
14041591...................$17.99

148. BOB DYLAN
14041592...................$17.99

149. AC/DC HITS
14041593...................$19.99

150. ZAKK WYLDE
02501717...................$19.99

151. J.S. BACH
02501730...................$16.99

152. JOE BONAMASSA
02501751...................$24.99

153. RED HOT CHILI PEPPERS
00702990...................$22.99

155. ERIC CLAPTON – FROM THE ALBUM UNPLUGGED
00703085...................$17.99

156. SLAYER
00703770...................$19.99

157. FLEETWOOD MAC
00101382...................$17.99

159. WES MONTGOMERY
00102593...................$22.99

160. T-BONE WALKER
00102641...................$17.99

161. THE EAGLES – ACOUSTIC
00102659...................$19.99

162. THE EAGLES HITS
00102667...................$17.99

163. PANTERA
00103036...................$19.99

164. VAN HALEN 1986-1995
00110270...................$19.99

165. GREEN DAY
00210343...................$17.99

166. MODERN BLUES
00700764...................$16.99

167. DREAM THEATER
00111938...................$24.99

168. KISS
00113421...................$17.99

169. TAYLOR SWIFT
00115982...................$16.99

170. THREE DAYS GRACE
00117337...................$16.99

171. JAMES BROWN
00117420...................$16.99

172. THE DOOBIE BROTHERS
00119670...................$17.99

173. TRANS-SIBERIAN ORCHESTRA
00119907...................$19.99

174. SCORPIONS
00122119...................$19.99

175. MICHAEL SCHENKER
00122127...................$17.99

176. BLUES BREAKERS WITH JOHN MAYALL & ERIC CLAPTON
00122132...................$19.99

177. ALBERT KING
00123271...................$17.99

178. JASON MRAZ
00124165...................$17.99

179. RAMONES
00127073...................$16.99

180. BRUNO MARS
00129706...................$16.99

181. JACK JOHNSON
00129854...................$16.99

182. SOUNDGARDEN
00138161...................$17.99

183. BUDDY GUY
00138240...................$17.99

184. KENNY WAYNE SHEPHERD
00138258...................$17.99

185. JOE SATRIANI
00139457...................$19.99

186. GRATEFUL DEAD
00139459...................$17.99

187. JOHN DENVER
00140839...................$19.99

188. MÖTLEY CRUE
00141145...................$19.99

189. JOHN MAYER
00144350...................$19.99

190. DEEP PURPLE
00146152...................$19.99

191. PINK FLOYD CLASSICS
00146164...................$17.99

192. JUDAS PRIEST
00151352...................$19.99

193. STEVE VAI
00156028...................$19.99

194. PEARL JAM
00157925...................$17.99

195. METALLICA: 1983-1988
00234291...................$22.99

196. METALLICA: 1991-2016
00234292...................$19.99

For complete songlists, visit
Hal Leonard online at
www.halleonard.com

Prices, contents, and availability subject to
change without notice.